The New Kite

Written by Julie Sykes

Illustrated by Ley Honor Roberts

Collins

Lenny got a new kite for his birthday.

Mum took the children to the park to fly the kite.

Tim said, "Don't let go!"

5

Lenny didn't let go of his kite.

Nina said, "Don't let go!"

Lenny didn't let go of his kite.

Mum wanted a turn.
Lenny said, "Don't let go!"

Mum said, "Oh, no!"

The children jumped in too.
Mum said, "I didn't let go!"

It was time to go home.

Dad said, "Did it rain?"

13

A Storyboard

Ideas for reading
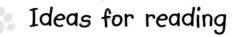

Written by Clare Dowdall PhD
Lecturer and Primary Literacy Consultant

Learning objectives: Use awareness of character and dialogue to read with expression; take note of punctuation to support the use of grammar and oral language rhythms; re-enact stories in a variety of ways; describe incidents or tell stories from their own experience.

High frequency words: a, dad, don't, for, got, his, home, in, it, mum, new, said, the, time, to, took

Interest words: kite, birthday, children, park, didn't, wanted, turn, oh, jumped, rain

Curriculum links: Science: Push and pull

Word count: 78

Getting started

- Show the children a kite, or look at a picture of a kite. *What do kites do? Who has seen one? Who has flown one?*

- Look together at pp2–3 and discuss the story characters – Mum, Dad, Lenny, Tim, Nina and the baby. *Whose birthday is it? How can you tell?*

- Scan through the story together, discussing what is happening in the pictures. On pp12–13, ask why Dad thought that it had been raining. Stop at p13.

- Find "Don't let go!" in the text. Model how this can be read in different voices. Ask the children to practise "Don't let go!", using a range of voices for reading.

Reading and responding

- Ask the children to read the story independently and aloud and, using their practised voices for "Don't let it go!", observe them reading, and praise appropriate expression and fluency.

- Remind them to use the characters' voices to make the story fun and interesting.

- As the children read, encourage them to decode challenging and new words by using the pictures and phonic cues. Model using p4, by looking at the picture and the initial and final sounds to help them read the word "park".

Returning to the book

- Look at the storyboard on pp14–15 together. As a group, recount the story from the dog's point of view.

- Ask the children to take you through the story again from the start, point out any challenging words and describe how they attacked them.

- Ask the children to demonstrate the voices that they used to read "Don't let go".

Checking and moving on

- Model retelling the story from the dog's point of view, using 'teacher in role'. Ask the children to choose a character and retell the story in role as Dad, Mum, the dog, etc.

- Ask the children to perform their recount to a larger group.